Be the **LIGHT** that **INSPIRES** others...

Brown Girl, Brown Girl, What Do You See?

WRITTEN BY: KISHA MITCHELL

ILLUSTRATED BY: MARIE PEARSON

This book is dedicated to Ansley, Brooklyn, and all inspired little girls; let your light shine brightly! And, remember, you can do ALL things.

Copyright © 2016 by Kisha Mitchell.

All rights reserved. No part of this publication may be reproduced, stored in a retrieval system or transmitted, in any form, or by any means, electronic, mechanical, recorded, photocopied, or otherwise, without the prior permission of the copyright owner, except by a reviewer who may quote brief passages in a review.

Published by

Be The Light Group, Inc.

4002 Hwy 78, STE 530

Snellville, Ga. 30039

Illustrations by: Marie Pearson

Manufactured in the United States.

ISBN: 978-0-9976219-0-7

As I gaze in the mirror loving the perfect imperfections of me; I see a confidence emerging that will not cease! I can feel my confidence increase!!

Brown girl, brown girl, there is so much more to see!

I see short, tall, curvy, and small, freckles, red hair....

Brown girls are perfect just the way they are; I know that I am the best me known to this world by far!!!

I am powerful beyond measure; UNIQUELY, CONFIDENTLY ME!

When I look into the mirror, THAT is what I see!